Moon Missions

Contents

Chapter 1 Mission launch................2
Moon map.........................12
Chapter 2 The Moon 14
Space inventions.....................22
Chapter 3 Space Race 24
Moon suit...........................34
Chapter 4 Gravity superpowers 36
Moon base..........................46
Chapter 5 Mission impossible 48
Chapter 6 Moon living 56
Amusing astronauts...................66
Glossary 68
About the author 70
About the illustrator..................72
Book chat 74

Chapter 1

Mission launch

Greetings, space cadet! I'm Astro, your guide on this mission to the Moon. I know the idea of flying thousands of kilometres across space to a massive lump of grey rock might be scary. But I can guarantee this trip is going to be *out of this world*!

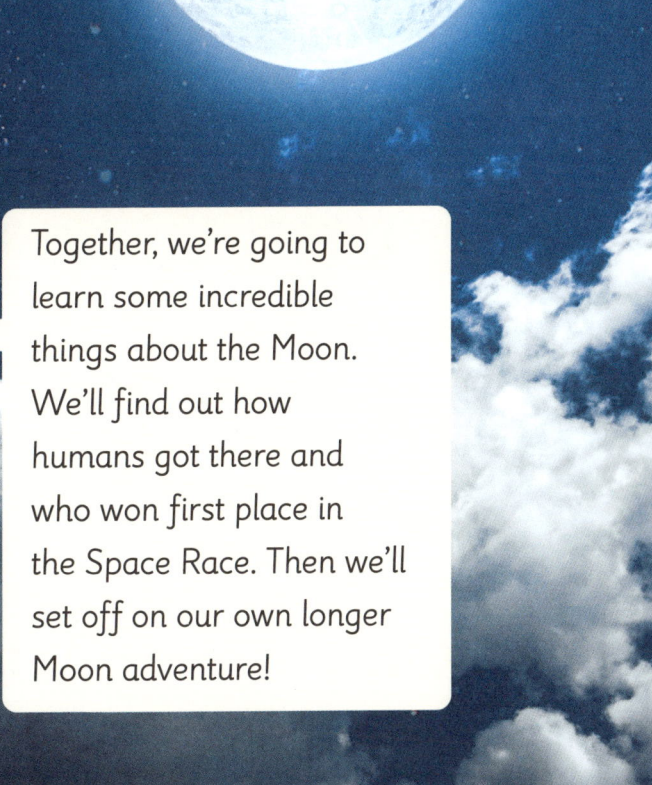

Together, we're going to learn some incredible things about the Moon. We'll find out how humans got there and who won first place in the Space Race. Then we'll set off on our own longer Moon adventure!

When we land on the Moon, we'll meet some serious challenges. I'm going to need your help!

We'll have to work out where to find water, and how to make energy. We'll need some way to grow food in space, and build a safe shelter.

We'll also explore what it will be like to live on the Moon. I bet you're curious about how hot or cold the Moon is. You may wonder what the Moon smells like, and why you might get lunar hay fever. And you'll want to know why you should *never* take your helmet off in space.

Well, we'll discover all that and much more as we jet off towards our destination. So, strap yourselves in and prepare for launch!

Lift off!

Taking off in a rocket is like being tied to a skyscraper during an earthquake. When the main thrusters fire, the whole spaceship rattles and shudders. A deafening roar fills the cabin. Then you feel a massive kick in the back as the ship blasts off the launch pad.

As the rocket speeds towards space, a force presses you down into your seat. This is **G-force**. It gets stronger the faster you go. In the 8.5 minutes the rocket takes to get from Earth to space, you travel from zero to over 27,000 kilometres per hour! During the flight, the G-force can be up to three times as strong as the **gravity** on Earth. This makes it difficult to move and breathe.

> The layers of gas surrounding Earth are called the **atmosphere**. The atmosphere is mostly nitrogen and oxygen.

You fly faster and *faster* and *faster*. Then, as your ship leaves Earth's atmosphere, the thrusters shut down and the speed suddenly drops back to zero. The G-force crushing your body vanishes. You feel an odd tumbling sensation as you start to float weightless in your seat. That's when you know you've reached outer space!

The whole experience can be really exciting … but we must be very careful, because one tiny mistake can result in a deadly explosion.

Stop the launch!

If it could be that dangerous, why are we going to the Moon?

I'm glad you asked, space cadet! There are almost as many reasons as there are craters on the Moon. Here are four key reasons:

1. To discover more about our solar system

Scientists can learn a lot by studying the Moon close up. By looking at the Moon's structure and what it's made of, they may find out more about how our **solar system** began.

2. To develop new technologies

Because of space travel, scientists have already invented lots of things that people use in everyday life. Did you know that the first laptop was invented to be used in space? New missions to the Moon could lead to even more brilliant inventions.

What do astronauts read for fun?

Comet-books!

3. To build a lunar base

A base on the Moon would allow scientists to carry out important experiments that can't be done on Earth. For example, they could study how plants, animals and even humans grow and behave in low gravity. Scientists could also set up powerful telescopes to look deeper into the universe, so we can study how galaxies, stars and planets form.

4. As a stepping stone to another planet

It's easier and cheaper to blast off into space from the Moon. This makes the Moon the perfect launch pad to reach Mars!

But we're getting ahead of ourselves. First let's take a good look at the Moon …

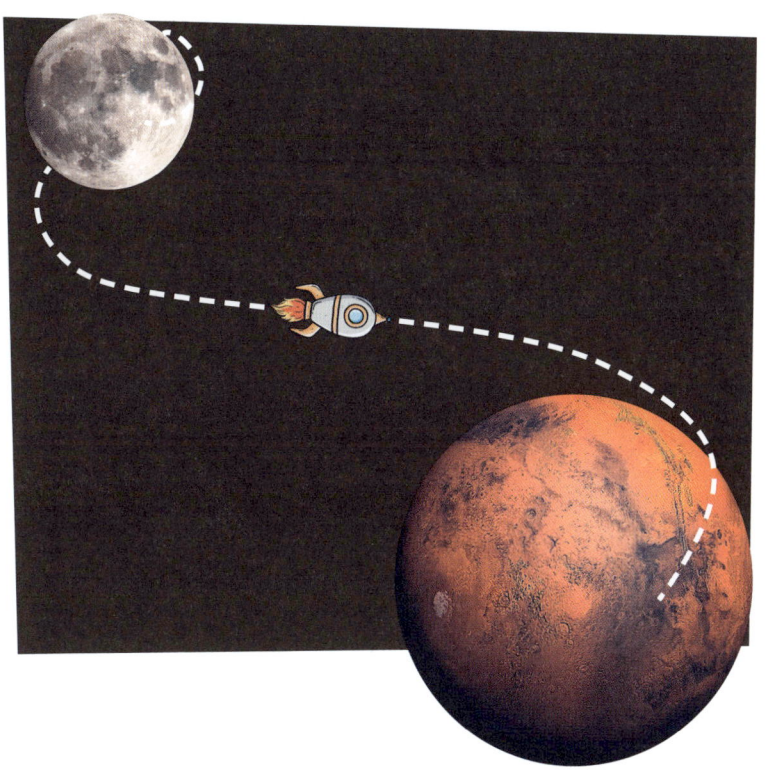

BONUS
Moon map

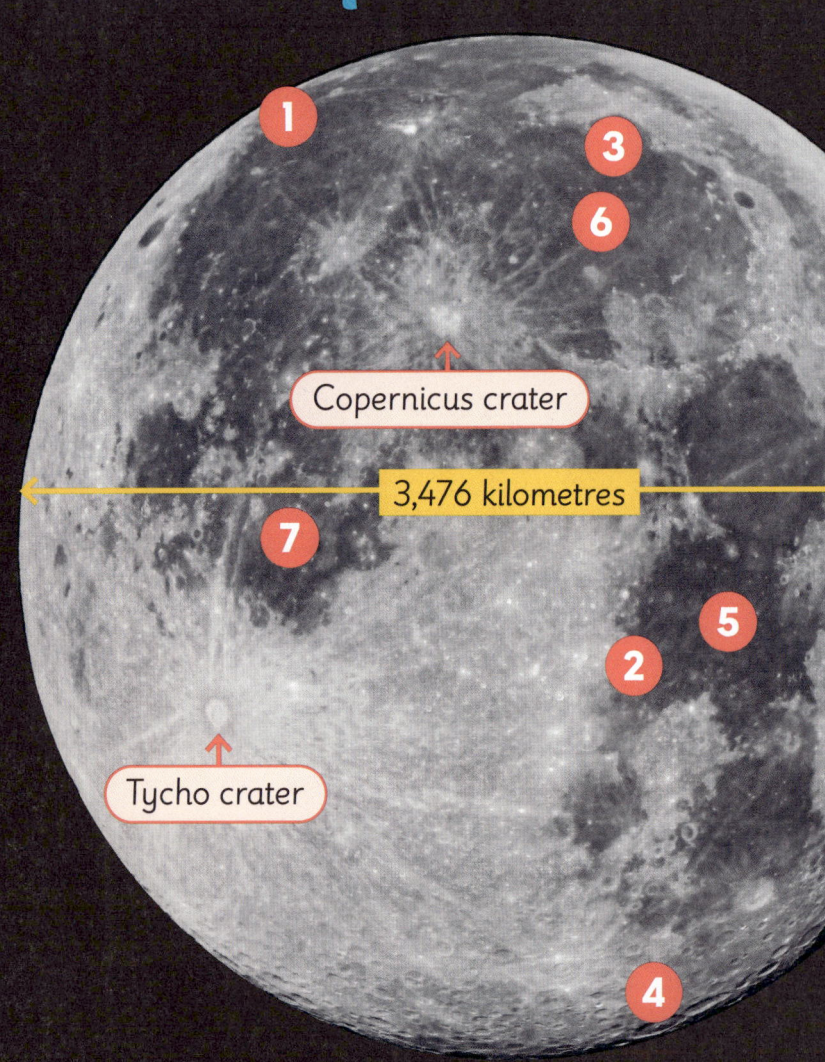

Landing sites:

1. The first spacecraft to land successfully on the Moon (3 February 1966, Soviet Union)
2. The first human Moon landing (20 July 1969, US)
3. The first spacecraft to land on the Moon since 1976 (14 December 2013, China)
4. The first lander to touch down near the lunar South Pole (23 August 2023, India)
5. Sea of Tranquility
6. Sea of Rains
7. Sea of Clouds

The Tycho and Copernicus craters can be seen from Earth without needing a telescope.

Chapter 2

The Moon

The Moon is the brightest and largest object in our night sky. Throughout history, its changing face has played a unique part in human life. Sailors use its light to guide their boats. Poets use its beauty to inspire their words. And astronomers study its surface to unlock the mysteries of space. But have you ever looked up and wondered where the Moon came from in the first place?

How did the Moon form?

There are various ideas. The main one is that a planet about the size of Mars smashed into Earth about 4.5 billion years ago. The dust and rocks from that crash came together, because of gravity, to make the Moon.

The Moon is a huge ball of rock, and it weighs a lot – about ten *billion* times more than Mount Everest!

Its surface is covered in craters from the countless **meteors** that have hit it over many millions of years. Some of the darker, flatter spots on the Moon are called ***maria***, which means "seas". That's because early astronomers thought they were full of water. But they aren't really seas – just huge craters that filled with lava a long time ago. The dried-out lava makes the craters look smoother than the rockier surface all around them.

The "seas" of the Moon have some intriguing names, including the Sea of Storms, the Sea of Nectar and even the Sea of Cleverness!

The Moon is shaped like an egg!

The Moon is over a quarter the size of Earth. This makes the Moon the largest **satellite** in our solar system compared to its planet. Other planets have larger moons, but none are as big as a quarter of the size of its planet. That's a brilliant achievement for an egg-shaped lump of rock!

From a distance, the Moon appears round. So it's natural to assume it's a big ball. But, the side facing Earth is a bit larger than the side turned away from us. This is due to the effect of Earth's gravity pulling on the Moon and creating a bulge. Over millions of years, this has turned the Moon into a very slight "egg shape".

The Moon is as bright as a light bulb.

The Moon may be the brightest object in the night sky, but it's no brighter than a 100-watt light bulb hanging 50 metres away. That's the same distance as an Olympic-sized swimming pool. The Moon only appears very bright compared to the dark night sky.

The Moon also isn't white. Its surface is actually grey. It only looks white because it's reflecting the light of the Sun. The Moon doesn't make any light of its own.

The Moon moves faster than the speed of sound.

The Moon is a solar system superhero! It zooms around Earth at an average speed of 3,682 kilometres per hour. That's almost three times faster than the speed of sound! As it **orbits** once around Earth, the Moon travels nearly 2.5 million kilometres. It takes just under a month to complete the trip – 27.3 days.

But the Moon doesn't travel in a perfect circle around Earth. Its orbit is elliptical (egg-shaped). That means the Moon isn't always the same distance away from Earth. But on average, it's about 400,000 kilometres away. This is about 30 Earths or the same distance as almost six million football pitches!

What do astronauts like to drink? Le-moon-ade!

So how long will it take us to get there?

That depends on where the Moon is in its orbit. The first time humans landed on the Moon, in 1969, it took about three days to reach the Moon. The 2022 Artemis I rocket took longer – five days, one hour, and ten minutes. But the current record for the shortest trip to the Moon is held by **NASA**'s New Horizons probe: it took eight hours and 35 minutes!

That's five minutes faster than it would take to fly from London, England to Orlando, Florida in the US! So what are we waiting for? Let's discover *how* we got there …

The Moon, I mean, not Florida!

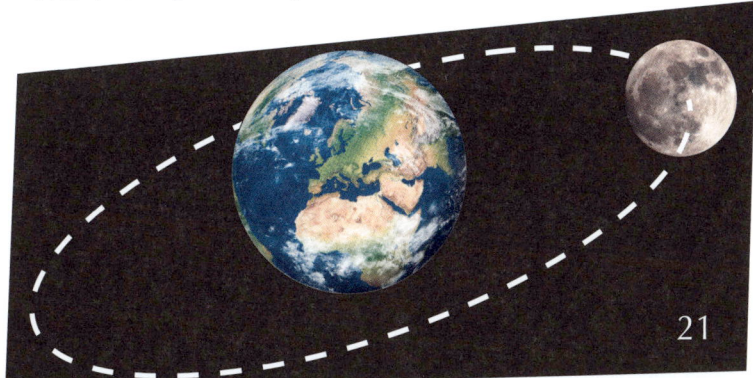

BONUS
Space inventions

Here are five useful inventions we have thanks to space travel!

1. Camera phones
Scientists needed to make cameras small and powerful enough to use on space missions. Now, that same technology is used in mobile phone cameras!

2. Dustbusters
NASA asked a company to make a small cordless drill to collect rock samples on the Moon. This drill was then turned into a handheld hoover that people use in their homes.

3. Freeze-dried food

NASA developed freeze-dried food for astronauts to eat on long space missions. Freeze-drying removes the water from the food, making it lighter and longer lasting. This way, astronauts can have meals in space without the food going off!

4. Artificial limbs

Inventors have created light, strong materials for use on space missions. Now these are used to make lighter and stronger artificial limbs.

5. Wireless headsets

NASA created these headsets so astronauts could talk to each other without getting tangled in wires. Now lots of people back on Earth use headsets like this too!

Chapter 3

Space Race

On your marks … get set … GO! And we're off to the Moon! The Space Race was a big competition between two countries – the United States and the Soviet Union – to see who could explore and conquer space first. You're probably curious about who won …

The first space traveller

The Space Race began when the Soviet Union launched a satellite called Sputnik 1, on 4th October 1957. Sputnik means "traveller" in Russian. It was the first human-made object to go into orbit around Earth.

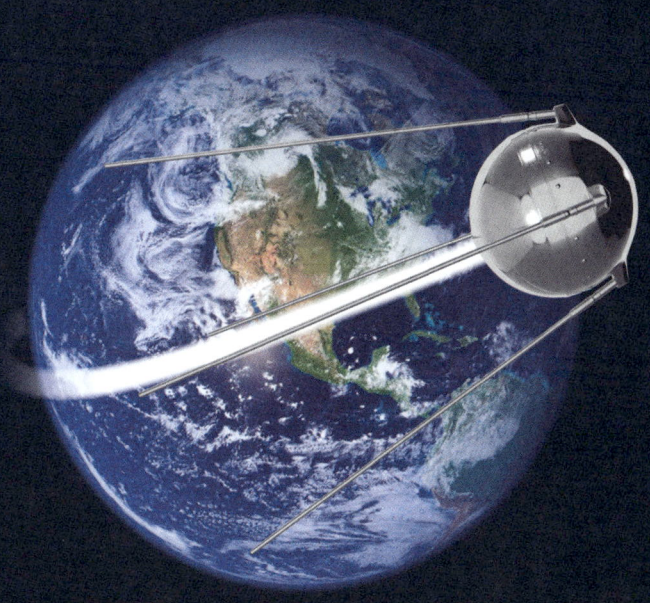

Taking the lead

The launch came as a big surprise to the United States and they raced to catch up. But the Soviet Union had the lead. Not only did they launch the first human-made satellite, they had many other space successes.

Russian space awards

First dog in space
1957

First spacecraft to reach the Moon
Luna 2, 1959

First man in space
Yuri Gagarin, 1961

First woman in space
Valentina Tereshkova, 1963

First spacewalk
Alexei Leonov, 1965

Space dogs and astro animals

Yes, that's right – a dog beat humans in the race to space! To begin with, no one knew what spaceflight was like. So scientists sent animals into space to learn about how spaceflight might affect humans.

The first animal in space was actually a fruit fly in 1947!

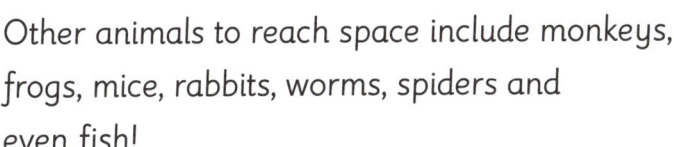

Other animals to reach space include monkeys, frogs, mice, rabbits, worms, spiders and even fish!

In 1973, NASA sent some small fish into space to see how they would swim in zero gravity. Instead of swimming in straight lines like they do on Earth, for the first few days the fish swam in circles!

Project Apollo

By 1961, the Soviet Union was well ahead of the United States in the Space Race. So, the president of the United States promised to land an astronaut on the Moon within the next ten years. The United States' Moon mission was called Project Apollo.

What did the astronaut say when he crashed into the Moon? I Apollo-gise.

Setbacks and successes

With Project Apollo, the Space Race hotted up and became much tighter. But the mission cost billions of dollars. Dozens of launches failed. Multiple rockets exploded. Several spacecraft caught fire or crashed on returning to Earth.

Then in 1966, the Soviet Union landed a small robotic spacecraft on the Moon, and sent back photos of the surface. A month later, the United States were the first to join up two spaceships in outer space.

Both countries were getting closer and closer to setting foot on the Moon.

Then, on 16th July 1969, Apollo 11 lifted off!

The Eagle has landed

There was no guarantee that the three astronauts on Apollo 11 would return from their trip to the Moon. In fact, they only gave themselves a 50/50 chance of survival!

After three days and over 400,000 kilometres, the lunar **module** – the Eagle – headed to the surface. But there were problems with the computer, and the commander Neil Armstrong had to land the vehicle himself. With only 25 seconds of fuel left, the module touched down on the Moon at 20:17 on 20th July 1969 and the commander announced, "The Eagle has landed!"

One small step

Soon after, the astronauts Neil Armstrong and Buzz Aldrin made their heroic first step on the Moon. Over half a billion people were watching live on TV. The United States was victorious – it had won the Space Race!

The race goes on

With the Space Race over, people lost interest in going to the Moon. It was simply too expensive and dangerous. Instead, the United States and Soviet Union worked together to build the International Space Station.

Over 50 years have passed since the last person set foot on the Moon. But now there's a new space race on! This time, there are more competitors – India, China, Japan and even some very rich people.

But there are still many challenges if we want to return to the Moon …

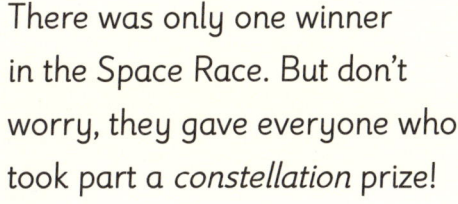

There was only one winner in the Space Race. But don't worry, they gave everyone who took part a *constellation* prize!

BONUS
Moon suit

A spacesuit is like a mini spaceship for the human body.

helmet:
- light band to see better
- gold visor to shield astronaut's eyes from the Sun's rays
- camera to live-stream videos to Earth

suit:
- lightweight and flexible joints for easy movement and bending down
- strong material to protect against radiation, sharp rocks and extreme temperatures

boots:
- thick soles to protect feet from sharp dust and rocks
- insulated to keep feet warm on the freezing-cold Moon

Chapter 4

Gravity superpowers

JUMP, space cadet, JUMP! I trust you returned back down to Earth? In fact, I guarantee you did. That's because of a force called gravity. If there was zero gravity, you would have simply kept on floating off into outer space!

The force

Gravity is the invisible force that holds us onto Earth and makes things fall to the ground. Gravity also keeps the planets orbiting around the Sun, and the Moon orbiting around Earth.

What's **mass?** It's the amount of matter in an object. Matter is the stuff that things are made of.

Anything that has mass has gravity, such as a rock, a mountain or a planet. The more mass a thing has, the stronger its gravity is.

For example, the Sun has *more* mass than Earth so its gravity is much stronger than Earth's. The Moon is smaller and has *less* mass than Earth. That means the Moon's gravity is weaker – six times weaker, to be exact.

I'm reading a book about anti-gravity. It's impossible to put down!

Lunar superpowers

The lower gravity on the Moon gives astronauts cool superpowers! Because gravity is six times weaker than on Earth, everything weighs six times less. This means on the Moon, you can lift heavy things you can't lift on Earth. For example, if you picked up a big dog on the Moon, it would feel as light as a small puppy!

You also won't get tired as quickly on the Moon because you don't need as much energy to move. If you fall, you're less likely to hurt yourself because you'll fall much more slowly. And you can jump higher and further, like a superhero!

Instead of walking, you'll need to learn to bounce or hop, just like the astronauts did on the Moon!

The downside of gravity

But the Moon's lower gravity also causes some problems. It's harder to stay balanced, so you might fall over more easily. Even doing something simple, like picking up an object, feels very different. Your brain will need time to get used to it.

Your face might puff up a little because the liquids inside your body move upwards in low gravity. Also, your muscles can get weaker, and your bones might become more fragile because they don't have to work as hard. That sounds a bit scary, but don't worry! Doing regular exercises can keep your muscles strong and your bones healthy!

What drink do aliens like to drink? Gravi-TEA!

Where has all the atmosphere gone?

On Earth, the atmosphere is made up of gases like nitrogen and oxygen. Gravity keeps these gases close to our planet. That's good news, because we need oxygen to breathe. The thick layer of gases also protects us from space rocks. If a space rock such as a meteor comes towards Earth, it usually burns up when it hits the atmosphere.

a meteor flaming through the atmosphere

But this doesn't happen on the Moon. Because the Moon's gravity is so low, gases easily escape and drift off into space. This means the Moon's atmosphere is very thin. That's why you can't breathe without a helmet on the Moon! There's no real weather either – no wind, no clouds, no rain. This also explains why the Moon is covered in craters. The thin atmosphere can't stop space rocks from hitting its surface.

Silent explosions

Another major difference between the Moon and Earth is that you can't hear anything on the Moon. On Earth, sound waves travel through the air to your ears – a bit like a ripple on a pond. But on the Moon, there's no air, so sound waves can't reach you. You might *see* an explosion on the Moon, or even *feel* it, if you're close enough. But you won't be able to hear it.

The Sun is one huge, continuous explosion. It certainly makes a sound, but the sound waves can't travel across space for you to hear. That's probably a good thing as it would be very, *very* loud!

Chapter 5

Mission impossible

If astronauts are going to live and work on the Moon, they'll need five basic things to survive. Air to breathe, water to drink, food to eat, a safe place to stay, and power to keep everything running.

Let's look at each of these problems and explore their possible solutions. Together, we can turn *Mission Impossible* into *Mission I'm Possible*!

Air

As we know, the Moon doesn't have an atmosphere like Earth does. That means there's no oxygen! So where on the Moon will we get our air to breathe?

We could transport tanks of oxygen from Earth. However, that requires lots of storage and would be very expensive. On the International Space Station, machines recycle nearly half of the air the astronauts breathe. However, more oxygen still has to be sent up regularly.

So one idea is to make oxygen from the Moon's soil! The soil contains a lot of oxygen. A special machine can extract this and store it so astronauts can breathe. By using this technique, astronauts won't need to keep bringing it from Earth.

Water

Without water, humans can't survive, so the whole mission fails. Since the Moon doesn't have rivers, lakes or rain like Earth does, where will the water come from?

Water is *very* heavy. The cost of transporting enough to the Moon for one person would be tens of millions of dollars a year! That's why much of the water on the International Space Station is recycled. In fact, a lot of it is filtered sweat and wee from the astronauts ... Nice!

However, ice has been discovered in the dark craters at the Moon's South Pole. The plan is to take the ice from these craters and melt it to get water.

South Pole

Food

Astronauts can't just pop out to the local shop for a snack when they're on the Moon. They need a guaranteed supply of food. To begin with, supplies can be shipped out. But for a long-term mission, astronauts will need to grow their own food on the Moon.

But this is a mission in itself. Plants require sunlight, water and **nutrients** to grow. Light isn't a problem, because we have the Sun, and electric lamps for the long nights. The problem is the Moon gets too hot during the day and too cold at night. So, we'll need special greenhouses to keep the temperature just right for plants to survive.

The Moon's soil also doesn't have many nutrients. We'll need to add chemicals to the soil, or grow plants in special water with nutrients in.

Greenhouses could be used to grow food.

Shelter

With no atmosphere, the Moon is a dangerous place to live. Temperatures are extreme, the Sun's rays can be lethal and meteors often hit the surface.

Astronauts will need special shelters to protect them from these space rocks. One idea is to use the Moon's soil to build thick walls to protect against space rocks and solar rays.

Another idea is to build the base in underground lava tunnels. There, the temperature is a chilly but stable −20 degrees Celsius. That's about as cold as a household freezer, but it would be possible to warm up the tunnels and live there.

Some people even think we could use inflatable shelters. Astronauts could pack these away tightly in their spaceship. On arrival, they could inflate the shelters like balloons.

Let's hope they are strong enough in a shower of space rocks!

Power

Finally, a Moon base will need energy to run all the machines, lights and life-support systems. The best solution seems to be solar panels. Since the Moon has no clouds, solar panels can receive sunlight during the day. Astronauts could use energy from the solar panels during the long cold nights.

Sun → solar panels → power

Mission possible

Building a base on the Moon is a huge challenge, but with clever solutions, the mission *is* possible. In fact, it's only a matter of time before humans might be able to live on the Moon. But what will living and working on the Moon be like?

Chapter 6

Moon living

Picture looking out of your window, and seeing Earth hanging in the sky like a giant blue marble. That's the incredible sight that would greet you if you lived on the Moon!

Long lunar days

Sunrise would be very different. Don't expect to see a soft glow on the horizon that slowly gets brighter. Instead, you'll experience an instant burst of bright sunlight.

Next, prepare yourself for a long day ahead. On Earth, we're used to a day lasting 24 hours. But days on the Moon are very different. They're called "lunar days", and they last as long as 29 Earth days. That's almost a month!

This means you'll be living in constant daylight for about two weeks straight. Your sleep rhythm will be messed up unless you block out the Sun in your bedroom. Then there'll be two weeks of night. It'll be so dark that you'll need powerful lights to see what you're doing. You'll also need special timed lamps so that your body sticks to its proper rhythm of waking up and going to sleep.

Hot and cold

The long days and nights also cause extreme changes in temperature. When the Sun hits the Moon's surface, temperatures can reach a scorching 127 degrees Celsuis. That's hotter than boiling water!

But when the Sun goes down, temperatures can plummet to −173 degrees Celsius. That's more than eight times colder than a freezer.

This is why you need to wear a spacesuit when going outside your moon base. The suit is specially designed to reflect the Sun's heat and also keep you warm in the freezing cold.

Lunar hay fever

When you do venture outside, one thing you'll notice is the lunar dust. It's everywhere! It covers everything like a veil and is one of the major problems of living on the Moon. The dust is super fine, almost like powdered sugar, but it's also sharp and sticky. It clings to everything: spacesuits, tools, vehicles and even inside shelters.

The dust can get inside machines and cause damage. Worse, it can make you unwell if you breathe it in. Some astronauts get "lunar hay fever" – sneezing, a blocked nose and a sore throat. Powerful air filters and special coatings on equipment will help reduce the problem, but won't remove it entirely.

And if you're curious … lunar dust smells vaguely like burnt fireworks!

See how the fine dust has made the spacesuit look dirty?

Where do astronauts go to catch a space train?
The International Space Station!

Keep a lid on it!

Now, if you're thinking about taking your helmet off to sniff the Moon – DON'T!

The emptiness of space will pull all the air out of your lungs in just a few seconds. You won't be able to breathe. You'll also experience a fizzy feeling as the spit on your tongue bubbles away. One person described it as like drinking a can of fizzy drink! But this feeling won't last long, as you'll pass out from lack of oxygen. You'll need rescuing very quickly!

A scary thought, and not a good way to end your mission to the Moon.

New mission

As we've discovered, a mission to the Moon is challenging and dangerous. But it's also incredibly exciting and important. If humans could set up a base on the Moon, we would learn so many things.

We'd find out how to survive in space for long periods. We'd get a unique chance to test new inventions. And the Moon would make a perfect launch pad for us to send rockets further into space than ever before.

You see, the Moon isn't the finish line in this new space race – it's just the beginning.

If we can learn to live on the Moon, we'll be one step closer to reaching new worlds. Are you ready for your next mission, space cadet? A mission to Mars!

BONUS
Amusing astronauts

Since a trip to the Moon takes so long, here are a few space jokes to keep you amused along the way ...

How do you throw a party in space?

You have to plan-et.

What do you get when you cross a lamb and a rocket?

A space sheep!

How do you store supplies on the Moon?

In crate-rs.

 What do you use to serve a meal on the Moon?

A satellite dish.

Why did the Sun go to school?

To get brighter!

 How do you put a baby astronaut to sleep?

You rock-et!

Glossary

atmosphere the layer of gases surrounding a planet

comet a large object made of dust and ice that orbits the Sun and has a long, streaming tail

G-force a force felt when a vehicle is travelling at very high speeds

gravity the invisible force that pulls a smaller object towards a larger object

maria Latin for "seas", large level rocky plains on the Moon

mass the quantity of matter which a body or object contains

meteors pieces of rock or metal from outer space that enter a planet's atmosphere

module a small part of a spacecraft used for a particular task

NASA the US government agency in charge of science and technology in space

nutrients substances in food that help your body grow, stay healthy and have energy

orbits travels around a planet, moon or star

satellite a human-made object placed in orbit round Earth or another planet, used to collect or 'send out' information

solar system the group of eight planets and their moons that orbit around the Sun

About the author

Why did you want to write about going to the Moon?

With new missions into outer space, I'm excited to think I may see humans living on the Moon in my lifetime. One of them may even be *you* ... this book is to inspire you to reach for the stars!

Chris Bradford

What surprised you the most during your research?

I discovered that tardigrades — also known as water bears — were the first animals to survive outer space. In an experiment in 2007, these microscopic creatures were dried out and orbited around Earth for ten days. When they returned, scientists discovered over half had survived the extreme cold, lack of oxygen and space radiation!

If you met an alien, what would you say?

I'd tell the alien a joke to make it laugh and show that I'm friendly ... How did the astronaut break his phone? He Saturn it!

What planet would you like to visit in our solar system?

Earth – this is our home. Our planet is truly beautiful and precious. I'd also love to visit the Moon to see what Earth looks like from space. We need to take care of our one and only planet.

Do you think there is life on other planets?

There are *billions* of galaxies, each containing *billions* of stars. Many have planets in the "habitable zone" – an area surrounding a star where life is possible. With so many stars and planets, it seems likely to me that life exists elsewhere in the universe.

Would you like to be an astronaut?

Absolutely! I practise "method writing" – I do what I write about. I've trained to be a ninja for my *Ninja* books. I've trained to be a bodyguard for my *Bodyguard* books. So the next natural step is to train to be an astronaut!

About the illustrator

What made you want to be an illustrator?

Pipi Sposito

Ever since I was little, comic books have always captured my imagination. One day I decided that I wanted to create my own stories. So, with paper and pencil in hand, I began to draw my own comic books! This was many years ago, but it marked the beginning of my passion for storytelling and the way that drawings can bring ideas to life.

How did you get into illustration?

Once I found out that drawing was a job that I could do for a living, I knew for sure what career I wanted!

Do you work on a computer or use pens, pencils and paint?

On this particular title, I only used my drawing tablet. However, I always have paper and a pencil to hand as it's the best way to create new characters (at least for me!).

What did you like best about illustrating this book?

In the past I've illustrated lots of books, but this is the very first time that I've had to illustrate a main character who is always FLOATING!

How did you decide how to draw Astro? Did you do research, or use your imagination?

I was inspired by real astronauts' suits and I combined their real elements with components from my imagination.

What was the most interesting thing you learnt when illustrating this book?

I was really not aware of how long a 'lunar day' is! Wow, I'd have so many more hours in the day to draw!

Would you like to go to space?

I would love to go as I am incredibly curious about what's out there. But I'd like to come back quickly as I'm nervous of missing my family too much.

Did you go to art school?

No, I didn't. I actually learnt by reading comic books over and over again and copying the illustrations until I was happy with what I had created. I really do recommend this constant practice as a great way of learning.

Book chat

What was the best fact you learned about space?

Would you ever want to go to space?

What do you think life would be like on the Moon?

Do you think life exists on other planets?

What was the most surprising thing you read in this book?

What would you find most difficult about living on the Moon?

What planet would you like to learn more about?

Do you prefer reading fiction or non-fiction books about space?

What skills do you think you need to be an astronaut?

Book challenge:

Design your own Moon base.

Published by Collins An imprint of HarperCollins*Publishers*

The News Building
1 London Bridge Street
London
SE1 9GF
UK

Macken House
39/40 Mayor Street Upper
Dublin 1
D01 C9W8
Ireland

© HarperCollins*Publishers* Limited 2025

10 9 8 7 6 5 4 3 2 1

ISBN 978-0-00-874637-7

All rights reserved. No part of this publication may be reproduced, stored in a retrieval system, or transmitted in any form by any means, electronic, mechanical, photocopying, recording or otherwise, without the prior written permission of the Publisher or a licence permitting restricted copying in the United Kingdom issued by the Copyright Licensing Agency Ltd, 5th Floor, Shackleton House, 4 Battle Bridge Lane, London SE1 2HX.

Without limiting the author's and publisher's exclusive rights, any unauthorised use of this publication to train generative artificial intelligence (AI) technologies is expressly prohibited. HarperCollins also exercise their rights under Article 4(3) of the Digital Single Market Directive 2019/790 and expressly reserve this publication from the text and data mining exception.

British Library Cataloguing-in-Publication Data
A catalogue record for this publication is available from the British Library.

Download the teaching notes and word cards to accompany this book at:
http://littlewandle.org.uk/signupfluency/

Get the latest Collins Big Cat news at
collins.co.uk/collinsbigcat

Author: Chris Bradford
Illustrator: Pipi Sposito (Advocate Art)
Publisher: Laura White
Product manager: Caroline Green
Series editor: Charlotte Raby
Phonics consultant: Catherine Baker
Commissioning editor and
 project manager: Emily Hooton
Copyeditor: Sally Byford
Proofreader: Catherine Dakin
Cover designer: Sarah Finan
Typesetter: 2Hoots Publishing Services Ltd
Production controller: Katharine Willard

Printed in the UK.

MIX
Paper | Supporting
responsible forestry
FSC™ C007454

This book contains FSC™ certified paper and other controlled sources to ensure responsible forest management.

For more information visit: www.harpercollins.co.uk/green

Made with responsibly sourced paper and vegetable ink

Scan to see how we are reducing our environmental impact.

Acknowledgements
The publishers gratefully acknowledge the permission granted to reproduce the copyright material in this book. Every effort has been made to trace copyright holders and to obtain their permission for the use of copyright material. The publishers will gladly receive any information enabling them to rectify any error or omission at the first opportunity.

p17 Science Photo Library/Alamy, p29 Allstar Picture Library Limited/Alamy, pp30–31 Granger - Historical Picture Archive/Alamy, p32 NASA Archive/Alamy, p35 NASA, p38 Mark Garlick/Science Photo Library/Getty Images, p43 Moritz Wolf/imageBROKER.com/Alamy, pp46–47 ESA-Pierre Carril/ESA, pp50–51 Stocktrek Images, Inc/Alamy, p53 Stephanie Jackson - Agriculture/Alamy, pp56–57 NASA, p61 NASA.

All other photos Shutterstock.